LUMINOUS
LOVES
GRAY

LUMINOUS LOVES GRAY

POEMS BY
BETH JACOBS

SHANTI ARTS PUBLISHING
BRUNSWICK, MAINE

LUMINOUS LOVES GRAY

Published by Shanti Arts Publishing

Designed by Shanti Arts Designs

Cover image—allec-gomes / 1xltymBTQ-Q / unsplash.com

Shanti Arts LLC
193 Hillside Road
Brunswick, Maine 04011
shantiarts.com

Printed in the United States of America

ISBN: 978-1-962082-72-3 (softcover)

Library of Congress Control Number: 2025940280

This book slid off the wings of the devas
Thank you
My life rests on the wings of my family
Ricky, Tara, Chris, Clay, and Zane
Also Sojun Diane and the poet sanghas
Thank you

Support for *Luminous Loves Gray* was provided
by the Lakeside Inn Artists Residency.

CONTENTS

APPROACHING

ENTERING

DIVING

SWIMMING

APPROACHING

THE LAYWOMAN

a monk came by the hut
while I swept dirt
where his brown sandals touched
the earth a lighter shade of the dust
diffused and where his heart moved
a similar trail of quiet widened
I nodded and brought out a pot
of grain with a wooden spoon
the weight of it all
like a baby on my hips
shifted as two spoonfuls
rose and fell to tap on the bowl
his eyes followed the ground
and the dome of his skull
was shaded with a dark stubble
imitating the moving sky holding clouds
I never saw his eyes
a smooth shoulder rotated by me
the faintest swish of old cloth
a vacuum force pulled my exhale after him
and a longing to know what he's seen
to be one bit as free as he is
of the noise and struggle
of the world of plain people
I hear a faint echo as I turn back in
and fabric brushes air where
I need to resume work and
feel the broom solid against my palm

READING SIGNS

on a short driveway
a hawk on a low concrete wall
and I startle each other
a few feet apart
creamy colored and bulky
she sends off awe waves
as her wide wings open
with thumb scallop edges
and she starts to ascend
glory turns horror as I see
a sideways wrapped cardinal
in her talons
the caught prey's wingspan
now a red dead cocoon

my son's psychiatrist told him
not to read signs in birds
and I know the problem
is the reading and not the signs
because it's not a clue
it's the truth I'd see
if my appetites
didn't rage around me
like flames licking on all sides
causing me to miss plain reality
and grab what I want
in sharp incisive claws

LIFE POEM

above all
be poetic
but don't drag
the feet of time
with description

my vow
of authenticity
includes knowing
exactly who
to imitate

if an interaction
ignites a new thing
it has value
in the universe
otherwise it is roadkill

being human
throws a veil
over experience
I'm so thankful that
it's made of tattered lace

CONCERTO

sometimes I think of Beethoven
being deaf with the most terrible
itch deep in his ear and willing to die
to hear ten seconds of his own
beautiful composition in the
salty air

I know he heard more than hearing
he saw it in every cell and tube
and vessel of his body in
colors he could touch
fingers on the pulse of states and
the shape of air

all of this biped vertical walking
as if we know the perpendicular earth
as if the path didn't melt behind our backs
as if we ever stopped crawling inside our steps
so blindly we glide unwittingly courageous
in the lucent air

GODDESS TRAINING

she met the night with a question
fear pushed her toes back
empathy cupped her heels
and brought her forward
she did not know
how many devas were helping
as the patriarchs kicked
her to the curb one after the next
she did not see
the ground itself trip her until
the dirt rose to meet her eye
in microscopic glory
every dust mote and loathed crumb
sang little songs in muted shades
told stories dense as myths
the curiosity of midnight
and love of reality
return to save
only the very lost

MEETINGS

whose crystalline
pattern remains
when we meet
like melting snowflakes
chest to chest?

the worst invention
in the history of interaction
is a weapon that
flings harm past skin
injuring without contact

staying receptive on approach
like a plane with
landing gear down
is a trained act
of necessary courage

we can circle forever
around the pine tree trunk
trading roles of
the Impinger and the Dented
crunching fragrant needles

every image is offered
and any will do
to convey across space
light's gift touching
life into motion

RENUNCIATION

when it drizzles
the volume of the day
gives away its space
to tingling grays
today cool air here
says give up summer
and remember
patches of atmosphere
hug this globe
like a raggedy quilt
somewhere it is so hot
the air is branding
babies skin
somewhere wind is so
volatile no one can catch
a molecule for breath
under climates lie
human-made or raw dirt
floors over the fires
of earth's heart
where weather stops
elements liberate

YELLOW-GREEN ORIENTATIONS

if I sit up on the dark green park bench
I can feel the ping and see the hail
of baby green tiny tulip maple flowers
each breaking off with just the right
proportioned stem for a fairy's bouquet

if I lie down on the dark green park bench
I can suddenly see the lacy dome of tree
has constellations of a flock of small birds
rearranging by the second as if the
night sky had suddenly sped up

if I tip the view enough times will the
hologram of awareness make
the unknown dimensions something I see?
And how is it possible that the
crudely built mind can dissolve gearworks
to recognize the wind and bird song?

A SEEING GIFT

two gulls
flashing against a gray sky
catching light
star rays of wings
turn
white sleek bombs
turn
flap of black dipped wingtip
gone
turn
sun harvesters of grace

it was the graphics
it was how silver is
gray with sizzle
mostly it was the harmony
wide set or shoulder to shoulder
one initiation of grand arc
through two bodies equally
and through two eyes
watching from the sand

SO MANY

as many as the grains of sand
on the banks of the Ganges River
they used to say
now as many as the stars in the sky
equal the twinkling neurons in the skull
as many as leaves as grass
as billions of people on a big ball
craving the same sense of warmth
that is inside the ball holding
another incalculable unseeable
amount of rosy orange light
like the sun's last breath on the horizon
for as many days as we've turned
as many as pixels in three dimensions lit
on the cusp of cascading splattering green waves
it's a pointillism universe in motion
before us the dots and through us the particles
holding is a laughable wishable notion
as many ionic exchanges as there are
on a square centimeter of skin
on the tip of a finger

END OF THE BIG GULP

barely oriented
trees are bearing down
with bare branches
to face winter's cares plainly
except the elm
bottom heavy
with yellow
and a refusing ginkgo
down the way
a woman in a car
poised at the red
jiggles her big white cup
and sucks on the straw
swirls and jiggles
tilts and sucks
we all crave one more drop

ENGLISH AS A LAST LANGUAGE

plain suburban birds
narrate my experience
in unintelligible flutter
swoop and tone
I'm forced to trust the untranslated
by witnessing various scenes
I cannot solve
like the dying cicada
wiggling on its back
swarmed by tiny black ants
it signals slowly with its legs
like an airplane taxi guider
imitating clock hands
with orange flashlights
who do I save
when I don't know what it means?
my down-to-earth partner says
everyone needs food
the wind says
you know nothing
the birds' crystal noises
ring from a broader perimeter

BLACK BOX

for Eric

I have heard from someone who knows
that frequently in black box recordings
there is someone who knows
that the plane will crash
but they allow deference to authority
to override their assertion
and everyone dies.
"Captain," they say, "I think there's a problem
here" and the captain says some
version of shut up
and they do and I do too

compliance and silence
are the team for any defense
against vague charges
and humiliations that hover
with stale fuselage odor
I am here to tell you Captain
I know there's a problem
and I'm not crashing again
in terror for your griefs
I have enough of my own
among all these crumpled wings
and mile high piles of debris

INCIDENT REPORT

threat makes the light on waves
beautiful and exhilarating
until someone drowns
IDs left on the beach
22 red metal trucks
of various sizes
with formal golden print
on their sides
could not save the young man
maybe helping the other three
maybe also caught in tides
those glittering surges
have caught me too
from before my mostly liquid
body was formed
as if protectable and whole
when I'm too exhausted
from grabbing up for air
I too will go
under and weightless
freed by water's seal
of every oxygen craving
surface and tubule
now all fluid
and completely fused

ANNIVERSARY

white furniture delivered all wrapped in plastic
to a little white house in the snow

one choice only, to hold or let go
and it's not even a choice

we used to flick playing cards across a room
slick at the flick then weakly airborne

tossing and rejecting through piles of image
where oh where is that one?

death's surprise one year ago
grief and I still circling each other in the ring

a wet wind holds the day together
an iron grip keeps me from flying apart

living with a gray cat
I should never forget the shadow of truth

MAKING DECISIONS

the different gods each have their own
                    invisible rain
some fall wetly
    some in powders too fine for sieves
            some drop in tiny round portals
            that open to clarity pockets
            leaving dream traces
oak trees are gods
    that drop shadows of thumbs
            pressing in damp dirt
the gods convene in clouds before the rain
their heavy bellies full
deciding who to drench in illusions of existence
            some laugh and
            some cry
as they watch them hit the skin

SARIPUTRA'S POEM

*Sariputra was a leading early disciple of Buddha,
noted for his incisive understanding and collation
of the teachings, as well as his gentle guidance of the
early Buddhist community. I have often wondered
about his personality and experiences.*

every night that I have that dream
I wake with a stiff neck
the garuda's brilliant green-gold wings
blot out the light and become sky
before they swoop at my head
hitting and clawing with forces
like rocks and knives and my hands
breaking the sacred mudra
also flap and fly around my head
to no avail

every morning no matter when I arise
the Buddha is already beyond
he is sitting on root rock or mat
the edge of his lipline turned up just slightly
his lashes the same amount barely hovering
over his smooth brown cheekbones
I sit beside him and warm waves wash me
of my nightmares and my day cares
and my particulars dissolve in rhythm
with no tremor

in some amount of time there is a scuffling noise
I crack my eye to one color tan that unfolds
into dust and feet and sandals and I know
that one has arrived and the rest will follow
despite all their care and mindful delicateness
I know each person by the sound of their sit
by the feel of breath through the shape of their back
by how they move air to find their dense path
and once it all settles we all breathe together
no difference

when the Buddha speaks my eyes open
though I hear with my feet and guts and heart
the words tear us apart and put us together
he speaks slowly and his accent rotates
with each person and every dialect
turning like a leaf dangling on a spiderweb
catching and dispersing sunlight abruptly
but moving lazily each word so pure
potent honey drop to the restless mind
with no residue

it is me who always breaks the spell
my hands, eyes and feet must all open circles
of mudra, view and men each time I stand
I feel splintered and blinded for one instant
of agitated confusion and organic rip
until from that point I take a first step
and the others follow like sweet ducklings
to my leading as we file by in homage
to the still sitting Buddha there on the ground
with no weight

I don't understand how the Buddha does work
but doesn't become it like I do
I hear monks' problems and sickness with worry
he holds them softly in his gaze
when I wash or mend the unwieldy robes
I become a person with cloth and tension in hand
I dip them in water and can't become water
like the Buddha who strolls without parting space
I hold the alms bowl while it holds him
no separation

in the fantastical evening the sun sets right through him
and I watch how the colors dim back and bow down
the beings of no form arise through the grasses
and lower from tree bark all around
sometimes I'm chilled and a heaviness sets
into my chest and I see days of my youth
joys of skin and mouth and bands of delusion
old hurts still misunderstood flare into fires
the garudas are flying and I keep trying
with no question

HOPE IS REALISM

for Doralee, Miro, and Susan

you can do this
you do know the feel of what's right
although it is so profoundly confused
with what feels like 'I'm' alright
you can draw from an inexhaustible source
because obviously something keeps universing
because ideas keep coming
and cells keep multiplying
and spring keeps pushing out even the doomed sprig
you can spread your undiminishable power
even if you can only wink one eye
or raise a corner of a lip muscle
you can do this
although we are all
adrift in forces we don't know
although the pain of error and loss is wrenching
and the terror of what's ahead is awesome
Why can we do this?
We know how to let this do this

ENTERING

SAXOPHONE PRACTICE

It is day two of Nariah's
acquaintance with her school saxophone
(feel how heavy the case is)
but she remembers how to put it together
and she can blow and some notes
are full with no edge of scratch
Her big eyelids down as she frowns
over what felted metal spoons
move what and she tells me
with a level hand chopping air
it's two high one medium one low
and she can blow right through
the pulsing tones that work or not
Her nine dyslexic years don't know
not to love what is new or not to
scoop in my approval as I smile
from the counter in the library
After a half an hour it was time
to get food with the other kids
so she dismantled and packed up
(Nariah put your sax back in your locker)
and what I am happiest about
is that I did not miss it because
I could have but I noted the moment
she could blow through the world's sadness

AVA

sitting atop a root-veined beach cliff
under a cottonwood and over aqua when
a skinny sandy brown girl pops
her head up and greets us
rappelled by a root and long legs
she heaves up to our ledge
and commences deep-eyed engagement
and stories and we talk and
doodle with fingertips in soft sand
Ava is adopted and her braids are frazzled
and her expressions are wild and
our exchange enchanting as sky
She draws a big heart in the sand
and I point out the flapping leathery leaves'
air dance with little hill shadows
of tans and grays inside it and Ava says,
"I know. I did it that way on purpose.
It has something to say."
When you meet a poet with a soul of gold
you can only pray out your gratitude with shiny eyes
you may remember the words but
the poem is lodged so deep inside
that your own veins become roots to the
next commonplace cottonwood miracle

COTTONWOODS SAY

twizzle sparkle flip flap flutter
swish swush wind drift matters
live love lights in glints
catch it lose it life's that quick
flizzle grain-beds dancing
molten leaf chips repuzzle
in greens of glorious flizz is shush

OAKS SAY

upright still leans and curves
my leaves move the wind
we're all so old and tired and strong
a deep furrowed hum song
the organ-rich hymn of blood and sap
I'm pure selflessness and I know you
more than you know me

LEVELS OF REAL

if all reality is a bubble
why do I love oak trees and feel hungry?
if pure mind admits no space or time
how did the booted lady just walk by?
if my self really does not exist
how do I tell my memories from his
and why did yesterday bear me
into today though I barely sleep?
if a zillion things happen per instant
how is the lake there and where
are all the fizzing drafts that I missed?
if the transcendent vows and visions persist
why this yellow button on my wrist?
and if not, why was the Diamond Sutra
on the park bench where I stopped to sit?

LIVE LIKE A POET

notice everything
don't waste words

SUMMER SAVES

I have some petty things to say
and I'm choosing another way
to go because it's that arbitrary
the confessionary so unnecessary
and the lyrics of this day
are in a branch's sway portrayed
in gray shadows on green
bouncing in and out of focus
saying what they mean
without needing a cortex
I am watching from the vortex
of pointlessness and love mixed
like objects in a twister
it's all so quick
today the breeze is so thick
and sweet and butterfly pairs
move with such aerodynamic care
they turn forty times
from right here to just there
and don't undo a thing
flashing graphic wings
perfect life allowing
freeing unconceiving
hot air so relieving

ONE LINE UNDER

under the good lines are the true ones
and under the true the pure
in the jagged aquifer is sweet water
which bonds together like people linked
by bent elbows or shining hearts
under the pure lines are the no lines
every line is an arrow pointing there
See? See? the calla lily's throat disappears
where the blue planes of lake and sky do backbends
against each other and peel away from the eyes
together as plain as two sheets lie on a bed
now we rest too and eyelids close over a globe
slither in between the quiet lines and be full

THE GRAFFITI ARTIST

for Clay

Index finger presses the nozzle
while the hand holds the can
in a fondle of color
and the arm moves through air
as thick as gold honey
and kisses the flesh of the wall
with wet paint and a plié
a touch so light and sure
should be reserved for the pure
but it's sprayed in dark illegal
caverns and city canyons
making urban the raw brick
making human the building
making a radial dispersing demigod
of the human

AFTER PORTUGAL

for Tara Louise

my daughter
forced into understatement
by her effusive mother
really hugged me back
at the airport
"it was a good trip"
my daughter said
forced into monosyllables
by her literary mother
I still feel the warmth
of a little girl
with golden eyes
round cheeks and a wicked temper
turning punk rock
and leaving me pet rats
to care for
when she went to art school
she looks like a cherub
and hunts like an eagle
she is fast and elegant
round and capable
under it all I feel
our soldier camaraderie
our sharp-eyed sharing
where things meet
we said goodby

POETRY AND PURPOSE

why do this?
at some moment
some you
is absorbing
through ears or eyes
yet I
alone now
in your past
scribble to you
I'm not exactly sad
but it's like I miss you
before we've met
and a corruption
chases the space
between us
such that I despair
of winning the race

why do this?
there is no life
in which I could do
anything else
I have tasted
the vagaries of the world
and can see how
the solvents
of our clumped up
tales and tears work
I scream Love You
out the window
to my partner
on a bicycle
never knowing
where a word trail goes
but wishing that this one
with butterfly flap
erratic zagging
wisps a portal to you

GUESS WHAT? THERE IS NO CONFLICT

for Kongyan Shi

the shadows of oaks
leave a signature mottle
here in the triangular park
where a couple fighting
on a bench behind me
left their teenage daughter
to sit sullen somewhere else
I recognize the terrible tug
for being believed
in the woman's ripped voice
I know the childish and sheepish
slump of the receiving shoulders

earlier today
a marvel of a tiny monastic
woman visits my back yard
and we share fruit salad
I am wide-eyed and ask about
her fluid clarity and she says
'I follow conditions'
awe ripples through me
from her certitude

the range of the human voice and heart
and the myriad lessons to be taught
by the gnarled wisdom and stonefroth grace
of arched oaks and life's ways
stretch past horizons
on one summer day

OFF BRAND LABELS

consciousness is being passed off by its states
like a cute baby at a big party
wishing for big-handed smooth uncle
but always by way of smelly old lady

this baby's body is a habitat
with a name on the map
border patrol quit ages ago
under the dirt there are no lines

a name gets slowly occupied
the population always in flux
only in death does it become fixed
on granite or Last Known Address

and still life feels so full
every dip into emptiness
lowers the bullshit average
black maroon maple leaves seal the deal

OUR SPECIES

language and imperialism are not human domains
listen to a bird or watch one chase another
off of a branch or wire
it's how much we weigh inner and outer
and feel like it matters
that marks us
maybe the alpha ape enjoys bossing the others
but first dibs on the food and mates
seems like the whole issue
human awareness itches to invade and control
the fire of association's quick kindling
sizzles lightning trails

because of the waft of sober truth showing
that inner space and outer space are
not just equal but identical
the inner eyelid dark screen breaks open
into a void where little suns beckon
straight ahead
and humans venture in by slipping out
of skin and words without ripples

BOUNCE

I crave the quiet core
while simultaneously grabbing for
mind carbs and munchies like
my lists and reminders I exist
and ways thoughts make time
feel so real
like rails make the train
play a thick picked song
of continuously thumby bumps
I've touched down
a thousand times
below all this
and bounced back up like the
flimsy beachball I am
pied in red white
blue and green fat slices
only an awkward valve
between me and extinction
Is it so much to ask
to remember under duress
that things I don't know
flow on into love?

KARMA GOT ME

I am an innocent bystander
of my own birth
as we all are
My slimy head landed
in fate's sure hands
cradled in their cup
and held until
those little shoulders
wriggled through
and the line of life
was drawn in plasma

As the cord to the host
is cut
intention to
survive whole
rushes forth
with invisible
but definite vector
The first surface
that geyser hits
is the virgin deflection
from purity

From there
the innumerable
'subtle and gross'
impingements on a life
shape a force
and create its ways
of dodging and flowing
folding into rose petals
emoting over the random
growing in tumored clouds

Always under
all that pinball bouncing
and ocean swells
the silent voice
calling us home
to what can never be known
before birth began

FAITH II

too molten to extract
too beloved to forsake
too transparent to seek
too blatant to miss
not just in every leaf
but in every tremble
of its dry or lit edge
in air's villages
the plain truth
will push the blind
through every correct
portal if asked

WORD FOR COLOR

some color you see is so sure of itself
it enters your eye without asking permission

there may be two and a half billion people on earth
sleeping right now easy and vulnerable limbs akimbo

every language bubbles and fizzes underneath
usually we merely ride its tonality

shadows as well as light holes in shadows
are not things but wondrous animations

a bird song or the rumble of a passing train
can equally pull up any bunch of words

there are joys imbedded in every leaf
ready to unfold into a transparent river

this river is washing our lives now and carrying us
to the white light that is all possible feeling ablaze

BASEMENT CLEAN OUT II

It is right to throw your possessions
in a heap that is bigger than you
It is good practice for death
or any time when meaning is unglued
from objects because no one is
there to impute
and hold them together
with wet forces
of projection and imagination
To catch a glimpse
of your mountain of things
is to begin to see
how the particles of shapes collapse
without the swirling forces
that coalesce in a life
The dried paste of specificity
disperses like smoke or sparkles
as every arrangement loses its angles
and all the curation
is wiped down to blank walls
Then the stuff will be bagged or boxed
and go to the thrift store or not
That it held together
with how it held together
will leave a slow-fading trace
in the shape of a dissolving hill

BASEMENT CLEANOUT III

the recycling from the basement cleanout
included maps from cities I visited
watercolors I did and loved once
and a construction paper pumpkin
with an accordion folded arm
and black paper hand that I held
as I dumped the box out
I rescued one other piece of child art
and shut the lid of plastic and heart

then the pressure inside builds
and I feel I could burst and splatter
bloody scraps of body tissue in the alley

but I won't and it will ease back
because I feel a truth and feelings for
reality move while feelings for stories
coagulate and boomerang
and the reality isn't just that
children grow up and trips end
but also that so much is missed
along the way in frazzle and constriction
in dead zones where all the life
landed only on the paper

PROSTRATIONS TO THE MIND DISSOLUTION
OF A BEREFT CHILD

for D. W. Winnicott

and to all children because this is part of it
and no one can remember like
no one really remembers falling asleep
or birth or death I suppose

Count backwards from one hundred and

See the hand zooming toward your face and

Watch the men carrying furniture out the door and

Hear the crack of the tree snapping and

Step over the edge and

you may find the words to wrap around it
but you still have to do the work
living with a packaged timeless emptiness
courting shy truth like feeding a squirrel

All I can do is donate moments
I can barely breathe in this realization
much less find an image to give
or a phrase to feed to hunger

Forget the poem
the child needs rescue
forehead to floor
you can steal your gifts back from the garbage

take them now while the coast is clear
the next time all context falls away
you won't blink
your worthy tears find a place to rest

TRADING CLOTHES

at the Frock Swap

I tie the graceful cords
in a bow on the back
of a stranger who has
chosen to try on
the light gray silk
designer nightgown that
Aunt Lois gave me
when I got married
I tell the woman
she looks beautiful in it
and she does
the desire for its liquid touch
and the body that was in it
and that version of sexy
has disappeared from me
I tell another stranger
about this and it makes me see
the good fortune
of desire's morphing
and culling and dimming
to a vague point
such scary blessings arise
from careful awareness
on many planes
with oblique intersections
I take only my empirical joy
forward and don't see
anything hanging
on the lines for me
the woman's eyes look
into her own eyes
in the mirror
as she turns
my little smile
lost and found
in her landscape now

GRASSES

Now the dune grasses and I
share the wind
many millions in a gaze
of green and gold
the multitudes of sharp edges
make a rolling soft
vibrato nod landscape
generous cottonwoods too
gulls camouflage in cloudy skies
all acknowledge air
in cool measure of
sideways power
bring more and more
and never run out

PATHWAYS

where we travel the trails close behind us
like we were diving in honey
golden and heavysweet
if butterfly wings cause tsunamis
here they woosh up black holes that
eat tsunamis for snack
even if you never step on one bug
your shape will leave a dent
in this liquid impressionable universe
getting it right doesn't happen here
relief and loss to realize
flow and mass to experience

CHANGES

as an elder I no longer expect
to recognize the products
of my pregnancies
I no longer look for comfort
in deliverance but stretch
acceptance's rubber glove
over all I've loathed
every item on the list
of things I know is translucent
the roadmap of a hidden world that
runs like blue veins under
taut flesh before the newborn
emerges in red noise and brightness
with such tender skin
and endearing proportions
all that is birthed
is a prepared surprise

PASTOR SAYS

"The day of your death is better
than the day of your birth." —Ecclesiastes 7:1

Because you left the park cleaner than you found it
Because you glide into sweet darkness instead of glaring light
Because you release release release diffuse instead of bleeding
       blinding bewilderment
Because all the energy of keeping the body warm and mind
       contained will turn into a sizzling sound of sparkle
       dispersal

But from the first moment of sensory soothing we suck suck
       suck so hard
But the exit signs are thickets and invisible arms keep slapping
       against the chest
But involvement feels like an anchor and since you don't know
       the sea its turbulence makes you vomit
But the glowing pulsing scarlet of a maple back-lit across
       the street is irreplaceable

The liberation and comfort war rages inside
Which is nevertheless more to the point than many other
       disguised battles and a good clear war is better than
       a reality snarl
I can ride through the noisy fray on a horse
while I decide which side to fight

8 IS FOR GRIEF

if you count crows
you have to listen to the number
and I never met beach crows
but these eight here are a family

you have to listen to the number
and it spells out grief
that is under wave motions
under crows coasting with fingered wings

it spells out grief
on wave-traced edges in the sand
becoming flat mountain range script
drawn with a tremulous hand

traced edges in the sand recede
and wash away in the tide
that pulsates from afar
a rhythm of a bigger greener size

all washes away in the tide
it can be gentle or violent
a ninth crow might arrive
still the sadness knows what it meant

URGENT

urgent care is scary
even though I've trained
and worked on swimming in emptiness

roiling dim sparkle clouds
of gold and indigo inside my eyelids
dissolve with a thought

the body is a frosty shadow
of itself in waves of light and air and heart
only the thought has density

the strangeness of sickness
invades more than the cells or functions
I feel my own unknownness

a diagnosis is its own relief
at first a snug rope belt cinched on a waist
and then becoming a leash becoming a noose

the rule-out is your invitation to step
off the hangman's platform for now
for joy for dispersal for the grand wisps of life

TOO REAL TO DEAL

Where are all the amoebas
and other realities
we learn in technicalities?
I believe in the amoeba
because I can be one
but I've never seen one.

DIVING

FINDING A RIDE

there are almost 8 billion of us
human body-located hotspots
of concern and intention
amidst incalculable numbers of beings
all of their poems
press my body into its shape
in proportions of despair and hope
all of the poems
filter through teeth and leaves and light
we are the crosshatches of feeling
writing how right now
I ride clouds of lost
and found destinies
the misplaced finds
its way elsewhere and every color
is in every other and so there
is nowhere to go but true
in the deep channel running through

A BROKEN MATRIARCHY

my mother's last decision
wasn't even to marry my father
because he decided that for her
so maybe it was to accept
the blind date or maybe
a first kiss
but it was the last
giggling openness
she would ever know
taken from her family
and home and mind
to places where rules broke her
with zero support
she became seaweed
and her children floated
in a cluster with her
unanchored unrooted
barely formed or notable
in our green in greenness
of a turbulent sea
it was so long ago
I still taste the salt
overriding the osmosis
of tears

SHAPE MAKING

when the smoke clears
what's left still looks like smoke
shape is so malleable
intention just one sculpting breeze
among many
tugging and punching in
and twizzling bright semigrays
Back when cigarettes
were objects of intrigue
I recall my grandmother
sucking rivers up against gravity
into forbidden nostrils
then magically expelling
suddenly-milk clouds in the room
Such power was reserved
for only her punctuations
of tensile crust family gatherings
As soon as I could strike a match
I followed her lead
but I smoked so hard
I missed the room
and only now see
the shapes we didn't blow

SLOW TURNING

those who persevere in dissolution find
that it is severe out here where all the air
seems to move through cones to siren
a world going berserk in its own detritus
like Jimi Hendrix and the supposed vomit
but I like to think he dispersed
in a chord of his own light and
the ancient Vedas agree

the fires and floods and winds
holding oceans like bowls rise up
but don't destroy the highest realm
of beings who float self-radiant above
every world system and maybe even now
purity is ascending like that to await
redeeming redistribution that is coming
in this shuffle that feels interminable

the luminous beings descend as the waters recede
to again mix golden seeds and mud into eras

FEAR OF DEATH ON ZOOM

I've never heard of it
but by now surely it has occurred
someone crumpling or tipping off screen
their rectangle remaining
when meeting ended for all
who would know what happened
or be able to respond anyway
living in another boxed room
bounded by another state or time zone?
so many deaths by or before screens
like the incarcerated now we all can fear
dying in a shape not a place
and dissolving only to one plane
not to sky or space or light

HOW MUCH MORE

the poems take longer to bubble up
and the bombs are coming quicker
marks of a degenerate age are here
apocalyptic disparities in species
the one who reads newspapers
and the one with shredded pieces
of others' bodies on his shirt
seventh time rehabbers and
sudden refugees
the cicada's
crescendo
shrill as a siren
under all sound
that equivalent rhythm
of desperation's sine wave
and the frequencies of faith
one third of the birds have died
which child will make it down the slide
which tree is left after the weird storm
what proportion of the forces we don't see
will deform our bodies and transmute love

WHO KNOWS

all the brilliant theories
and information gems
glitter before me
like the light on little waves
twinkling white against green
but I have to get wet

the sturdy railroad tracks
cross hatch to the horizon
in gorgeous clarity and symmetry
you haul up onto the train
or spend your life eating
from the station's vending machine

I hate the feeling
of untaping my self from my skin
the premeditated sting and ways
raw air hits all over
I'm not a content amoeba
I'm a working embryo

STREET POETS

the great masters of formlessness
used manual typewriters to peck
iambic pentameter among pigeons
on tables at city intersections
I've seen them on the corners
and received their healing poems
for lost children and skies
from city to city they chase
the tail of pain's dragon
with their balm of gooey letters
in cloth packets tied with string
the offering placed at the foot
of the demon appeases for a bit
but the one flung into a black well
finds its purpose point blank

RHYTHM

words live in space
like we do
but their exchange
is not air
moving in and out
like a pulsing blob
instead
words throb
with the potential
of being infused
with one aware drop
of a heart
going achey
or sour
or swollen
from life
word awaiting waves
of loveload
like faces
toward light

TWO USEFUL THINGS

scissors snip and spatulas smear
both important in the granularity
of an ionically charged sphere
the scissor gets between it all
and brings alive found lines
widening vees and growing
the potential of space inside
anything while my silicone
spatulas dissolve difference
and resistance to covering
and turn blobs into intense
planes of pointillism
if I could be one I couldn't choose
wisdom grabs the true tool to use

ODE TO A FOUNTAIN PEN

I've said it once and I'll say it again
My favorite thing is my fountain pen
The nib is gold and silver and
the elegant shaft melts in my hand
In microscopic detail a Celtic knot
is carved in the nib and floats to the top
and the F for fine point is tucked under the lip
The cool blue ink always flows hot at the tip
It's mysterious and never falters
with vital juice to bursting letters
Never a scratch, not a blot, a regulation
that follows and makes a trail of curation
of heart and magic where they meet on the page
The pen is the prism where forces engage

GRAVITY V. CONSCIOUSNESS

gravity is how matter meets matter
consciousness is how mind meets object

we cannot see gravity
but we rely on its effect
with great precision
every time an eye blinks

we cannot know knowing
just its vast array of objects
abstract as a word
or sensory as blueness

we use gravity to stack boxes
we use consciousness to whip up thoughts

great engineers employ gravity
to design huge buildings and bridges
that span space and house bodies

great poets knead consciousness
to pull language up from heart
changing air into intimacy

FAMILY PHOTO

there is the one that sprays you in the face
like a skunk and says truth truth truth
after you can stop blinking
your face as a child floats
off the surface and starts haunting
your days and dreams and dangles
over the abyss where you dismiss
it and interact as if it doesn't
exist inside your every cell and thick
feature and curve of a cheekbone
Still she lives and still she was
frozen outside of the circle of love
but that little game face had the half
smile of knowing and holding on
it can still soften the moment
with a trace of smooth skin
touching the underside of
time's chisels and patterned pores
tiny survivors frozen in photos
with grace's backward image reflection
changing left to right

PERSPECTIVE'S PUNCH

when my sister died
suddenly all this wet juice
drained from our connection
like a drop of ink drying
and losing its brilliant blue light
or the wave receding on sand
and pulling back all its glow and coherence
and what was left
was matte and plain and sad
because I missed so much
while squinting in the flashing glint
and while drenched in old things

when it's over
all the gummy viewpoints released
the truth below them
emerges like a shipwreck
in a diminishing tide
or like a triangle dice face
in an old magic 8-ball
saying "ask again later"
the clearer the view
the less answered are the
questions I should have
asked before

I DIDN'T MEAN TO BE HOUDINI

but I woke up underwater with my ankles tied
and my wrists bound behind my back
I woke up with an impossible necessary next breath
I got squiggling quickly

Houdini seems to have had a wholesome family
although he turned to magic to make a dime
to support his unemployed rabbi father
in unlikely Wisconsin

Scotland Yard couldn't secure him enough
a full beer barrel didn't drown his escape
he started magician societies and publications
he was a pro

I feel a connection in our shared Hungarian blood
although for him maybe it didn't feel so abrupt
there's a shocking moment when realizing you're trapped
is the only freedom

finally the huge gasp in open clear air
the shake of heavy chains off the aching hands
it seems like it ends with the infusion of breath
until the next

COURSING

Inside all this gray
is a vivid shimmer
and I'm begging you to
bring your eye to the keyhole
make the room a minaret shape
and witness the lonely ghost
trailing ink
like lines in the journal
of a dying girl
chemicals inside her
from handfuls of pills
slapped to the mouth
exploding among cells
the pain is an internal
loop from gut to mind
the last breath
an exchange
from the magnetism of core
to the gratitude in diffusion
from collection to context
from source to new source

THIS ORIENTATION

a strange light is growing
it is in the air
and mounting
the yellowed milkweed leaves
but I cannot tell
if it comes to me
through eyes or skin or mind
today the senses are in disarray
the monk told me
that ignorance will outlast
the mountains and the evaporation
of the greatest ocean
the vastness of that truth pounded
like a gorilla in a shoebox
but I can't let it out
my heart is dissolving
despite umbrellas
doors are opening
despite gone buildings

APOCALYPTIC APOTHECARY

The pigeons can still turn as a crew
and slice the light in unanimous wings
but the humans have lost the join of formation

Anonymous became alienated
not the fun feeling of walking
down a crowded gum-splotched
sidewalk in a big real city
strolling free of characteristic
pure quirk and intention like everyone else

Now we all scream Liar
with the exact equal outrage
our faces and jabbing fingers
in every radial direction
Bitter injustice is the shape
of every calling card
slipping through the ether's net
It's so lonely out here now
that we've wed robotics
and stylized the tantric forces

Under speaking sparkling trees
is the prescription of old trust
and the model of underground root gangs
with longevity and negative wanderlust
It's so loving in an afternoon park
knowing it can all go away

CESSATION III

*The cessation of suffering is the third Noble Truth
of Buddhism, deceptively simple in language.*

There's nothing to stop
Or no one thing to pick out of it
Suffering ceasing?
seems like it's all proportion
and course corrections
carefuller spice of recipes

CESSATION IV

clouds drift to the left slowly
a new sky per window frame
occurs maybe every minute
while a silver plane shoots right
like a needle in a vein
the gray cat rearranges
gelatinous mass in fur
we both gawk at fall's last fuzzy bee
flying through chips of green light

and so good fortune beckons me
while my sternum remains in free fall
from feeling the plane crashed decades ago
the cat condenses his sprawl
stretches and leaves the desk
as if to say you bring the poem
home on your own
find four words to say
just alive just now

LEFTOVER QUESTIONS

from where could the terror
of an unlocated self arise?
first a warm rush
from the throat of space
then a million radial tendrils
flutter for contact
and every trapeze artist
misses the connect
without a net

why does the restless traveler
have a phobia of the capitol?
the imperialism of consciousness
is so evident and agile
stealthy trapper so well equipped
lay down the metal pick and clip
and slip out of the furry parka
to step naked on ice
nothing left in the repertoire

is it a wet circle of sadness
or a sad circle of moisture
around the eyes?
evoked by the beauty
and insecurity of floating in space
every known phenomenon
is a lightning rod
to the devastating jolt
of a quickening beyond time

YOU CAN'T PROVE ANYTHING

for Nina

the frustration of the sane in crazyland
is a raging fire requiring fat helicopter
loads of forceful water to contain
but it never goes out or cools

that prescient child with churned up parent
feels it in the neck straining forward
because they can't explain the obvious
or join the charade parade of platitude

sometimes even the trees we don't believe
must stamp the feet of roots in soil
watching us running like squirrels
only with less efficiency and purpose

how the angels must squeeze their fists
and saints gnash teeth and devas cry
at times but they keep sending
the invisible notes of tune and paper

reminding us we know and forget over and over
sending twinkles up and down spider webs
holding our attention until the ink dries
for a moment of truth to ease the deep sigh

SWIMMING

OPEN CIRCLE

the difference between floating
and free fall is just vertical wind

wind is just traffic
in the invisible

the invisible is a translucence collection
lingering inside light

light flushes out of space
where there is welcome

welcome is the sky's smile
without a lipcrack of difference

IT'S NOT EASY

Love's cost
is the solitude
of total allowance
of the unaware

Your best painting
masterpiece hung
in the museum
of the blind

Your jewels
slipped through fingers
on a dark street
on a rainy night

Love not pure joy
Hate not equal evil
love more release
while hate can clutch

It's not just
you let go
but you do so
and no one knows

You give away
the boat
and float

ADULT CHILDREN

the sky recedes from itself
in ridges of blank whiteness
the same wave lines piled
up on a beach
carry love water lapping
in my heart for my children
when they visit
we run to foreign stores
and eat candy in
only the best wrappers
with funny colors and characters
we have always done this
to share the world's goodness
and find treasures
that both reflect and question
what we've been for each other
something never known
something opaque
it accrues in a constant layering
of fun and disappointment and longing
forever tumbling over themselves
between amber moments
of eyes meeting

BLUE GLASS

make plans
just know
they can shatter
into hundreds
of cobalt blue
glass shards
like the soapy plate
I held
in one hand
that exploded
with a weird
friendliness
missing the cat
who looked
back at me
with widened eyes
like mine
and me with
a tiny chip
still held by
thumb and one finger

what fault line
ionic house-of-cards booby trap
awaited the perfect spot
of pressure turned trigger
applied in that moment?
the answer is broken
wide open like
my dishwashing idea
of what would be next
and will be

LAYERED

the astrologer said
as I get older
I will get younger
but not quite
as I get older
I get less
I'm fading finally
and finely
like the purple fist
of iris curling into
a brown tissue-paper
wad after starting out
two dimensional
as a green sword blade
wisdom's arrival
unbidden meets
a million layers
of rippled habit
and nails truth
right through
naming the unknown
and loving the unnamed

WALKABOUT

Right this minute the day is changing clothes
the chipmunk and I both look up
at the slightest pinpricks of water
as the light goes so gray that a terracotta urn
starts blazing its color like an announcement
it says This is the end of the sweet warmth
the high branches nod in agreement
I dream of packing all the time but this trip
requires a dispersal of provisions
leaving picnic baskets and old suitcases
piled in a jumble like on Ellis Island
where I shivered feeling the hands
of my ancestors on worn brown handles
when it's time to diffuse even the mightiest
vindications won't matter and decades ago
the jury yawned and left the box
on this journey every version and verse
will sizzle into particle and sparkle
now there is nothing left to imagine

SOMETIMES THE FEELING

faith is a river of dawns
wide and slow or rapid
to behold its invisible light
to wash in its muscular currents
so wild and plain
let the winds take your hand
and your feet rest
on its cool bed

TILL

the difference between
sitting in a chair
and sitting at a desk with
a pen in hand and notebook open
is the difference
between plopped and poised
between laden and launching
between just there and aware
it's really not the words
it's waiting for them
rejecting a thousand options
examining potent details
angling this way and that
for the portal or gold of reward
a faint nausea of bodily urge
it's so quiet like snowfall screaming
before a poem

LISTENING SKILLS

my dreams are writing poems now
and trying to send them back to me
my waking self ninety nine point nine
percent oblivious mixes them up
with junk mail on the floor
recycling without reading until
maybe their millionth try
something so generous and persistent burns
with a sourdough incense smell
why wait so long to recognize
the embers of sustenance that I meet
with the kindling of my body and life?
extinction is not the end of the source but
the hint of imagination's birthing

in my dream I wrote the word vehicle
in caps and vertical like Michael McClure
an extra V on the bottom said it will start again
all the nonsense and violence riding me
along with the prescience and particulars
of every coasting metaphor in air
vehicle and purpose alighting right here

MONDAY POEM NOW

the late snows of winter arrive
with delicate bows and apology

while I wait for a line
furrows in tree trunks smirk at me

joy is an acquired state
I set an alarm to remember to have fun

I can't court relief just
dismantle the relationship to pain

dead stalks turn live with caps of snow
sway and gossip

I don't have to write a damn thing
until the thing tells me to

surfaces amaze me with their matte
generosity and tolerance

a purple bus advertising a cardiologist
can't stop the drumroll of truth

SHY MOVES

I've been putting my lists
in the coffee bean grinder
and mainlining caffeine
straight from the fridge

today all I read is written
more than two millennia ago
or by a person
under the age of ten

I'm courting freedom
and freeing ambition
with a c'mere
on the scale of fairy truth

protective meditations
unlike protective parents
kick me to the curb
achy behind and opened eyes

squirrels and rabbits
back legs land in fronts' prints
such precision of arc
such deception of trail

all the machines turn
the people invisible
handling wheel or keyboard
fingers emptier than glass

spring bird so miniature
can disappear behind a twig
afternoon sky so thick and soggy
like wet bread in a gray bowl

every detail so ripened
why do some hit so hard
upon the eye and heart
tremulous and unsure yet open

COLOR

I watched the rare indigo bunting
for long incredible minutes
as it hopped on the common old cement
outside the window
and picked at baby bright leaves
that grow in the cracks
I was looking hard and catching
details that scattered like seed bits
and debris rejected as the beak
of the beautiful bird probed and
curated its nutritional needs
I knew this visitation mattered
and studied it but I couldn't
shatter the distance until he turned
and flew and only in the bright winged
afterecho of a quick upflap
did the blue pierce through me

DIGGING IN

for Ricky

please don't mind
the particular words I use
to stalk the page
while a rose turns velvet
in afternoon light
I just want to feel lines
unrolling as the wind
tosses the compliant prairie
I want to stake a claim
in existence whatever it takes
but that ground is nothing
compared to the dirt we dug up
one blazing hot day
to make a prairie patch
cultivating wishfulness
with sprouts of bee balm, echinacea
and the ones we call popcorn plants
which grow so naturally
compared to my labors
to possess what I don't see

OPALESCENT

anger is crouching
lower and lower these days
and even the babies
are crying with a
switchblade in the fist
evil gods are
life-jacking back
where youth bloomed
while the old
work to remember hope
and hold it potent
you have to take a
teardrop off the bottom
of the glittering icicle
onto the tip of your tongue
and swallow hard
the prism splays
a rainbow in your gut
it's an unseen homeopathy
against darkness
when you speak
all the colors
flair out with your words

FULL AND MOVING

a strong wind throws the bright light around
if I followed so much as one fern's branch
I would know the universe and disappear
only our asynchrony makes it visible

if I followed so much as one fern's branch
I'd be the master of precision and detail
only our asynchrony makes it visible
the fern blasts more green light than I can see

I'd be the master of precision and detail
in a world of recursive and heavenly design
but the fern blasts more green light than I can see
as I flow in its quiet transparent sea

in a world of recursive and heavenly design
I would know the universe and disappear
as I flow in its quiet transparent sea
strong wind and tears turn the bright light around

WAITING WITH OAKS

their vibrant patience
is my teacher

their unabashed irregularity
is my model

their sweltering leaf dance
is my lesson

their transcendent humor
is my support

their stoic oakiness
is my heart

SONNET DEMANDS ITSELF

a crystal suspended by string
catches sunlight like an ace in the outfield
relays it to eye and causes exploding
one moment one angle this is the yield
retina to cortex much less than a second
body weight triples and freezes in sight
of turning pure colors reckless unbound
I'm pinned to the floor by feet and light
slowly then language starts to arise
like miniscule steam wafts from dew
that evaporates to return to the sky
releasing invisible patterned yet new
thoughts like the crystal is from my sister
who died and I still am learning to miss her

RIPPLE GHAZAL

I cannot remember a wave
I can remember its spray

    Why don't we have a holiday
    for how ripples on rocks match waves

        my cat and the heron
        same stalking advance of gray

            memory isn't a substrate
            it's the cousin of your guest in a play

        other beings seem to have steadier states
        we humans are so volatile that way

sand is so gracious
takes allness in and silently rearranges

      to love a wave is only to wait
      watch its influence break and replay

           shore lines and love lines and hair lines
           and poem lines exist to change

        a simple pale rippling
        is the doorway of grace

DARK BRANCHES

till you reach the sorrow with no basis
you will wander in the forest
of story and explanation
all the varied densities of green there
from baby leaf exclamation to earthen shadow
dizzying in their array and mosaic
turn like a kaleidoscope
though you think you walk forward
every path ends in a botanical snarl
when you sit and don't cry but dissolve
the pure sad changes places with you
who would own such pre-existing grief?
where would the little birds fly without it?

TIMES

sometimes my shoulders
turn to mauve-bellied mourning doves
and flutter off of me in symmetry

sometimes I am flying so blind
I crash planes and put on
my oxygen mask last

sometimes the narrative is
so justifying I miss
its quick switch and land in a ditch

sometimes forces help me stumble
revise where I'm going
arrive at floating palaces

other times solidity and diffusion
twirl like two ribbons of smoke
from a wide paintbrush

always oak trees are kind
life is more for real than good
the motion is rich

VILLANELLE FOR LAKE MICHIGAN

repeating ripples from sand to sky
tan where the green wave lets you see through
forms are reshaped in the swipe of an eye

there by the lake the day will drift by
erasing the moments you thought you knew
repeating ripples from sand to sky

you watch the horizon from where you lie
you turn the scene sideways like nothing is true
forms are reshaped in the swipe of an eye

sit back up and retilt with velveteen sigh
restoring the water and earth in your view
repeating ripples from sand to sky

a lifetime so mobile the trees seem to fly
and even the sunset cannot hold its hue
forms are reshaped in the swipe of an eye

there is no response to questioning why
take the gift of this moment and that broken one too
repeating ripples from sand to sky
forms are reshaped in the swipe of an eye

THE DEVA REALM

soft butter smears across the rocky tan toast
as pleasure can smear forward into time
if only you know how to stop making stuff arise
then the breezes are gold like honey
and the sunlight is thick like honey
and the mouth is dark sweet like honey
if only because the ratcheting gears
have gone silent and numb
and the tongue dumb of voice
and choice is never and yet open
so Venus steps on the half shell
her hair and flowers drift sideways
in fluid velvet breezes of nothing to close up
then the jewel chariots in transparent sky
move faster than thought
and thought is for joy
and joy is for anyone
and anyone is the only one there is

WIND

you rip my mind off
into your force and the branches
you move my hair
as if I'm young still
the trees heave and swoon
my skin disappears then craves you
you are the freedom and danger
of relentless releasing
I love how you let me go
I love how you carry
the lake's call all the way
to my ears in the morning
I love how you fill up
everything so I don't have to
I love your voice
swelling hysterical
then shushing romantic
I wish I was you
until it is clear
that I am

THE ENLIGHTENED DON'T KNOW IF WE ARE

night is coming on
already shadows dissolve
the sweet lapping of water
on the side of a wooden boat
lullabyes a trance
anyway who cares
if gentle currents
go this way or that
or turn rough?
we've been jostled
and leveled over and over
again and tonight
we float

tomorrow's eyes open now
to foresee daybreak and
breeze and light play
on waves and how
thin golden lines will
slither like fast snakes
under the surface

tonight's eyelids slide shut
and make a screen
for more movies of mind
the rocking and the
sizzle clouds of color
morphing in darkness
mesmerize again
we float
  above and below
    unchosen

BETH JACOBS is a lifelong writer of non-fiction and poetry and has published the following books: *Writing for Emotional Balance*, *The Original Buddhist Psychology*, *A Buddhist Journal*, and *Long Shadows of Practice: poems*. She has also compiled and edited four books of community poetry from her work facilitating expressive writing groups, the most recent entitled *The Sound of Unspoken Things: Poems of the Tuesday Writers Retreat*. For more information please visit her website: bethjacobsbooks.com.

www.ingramcontent.com/pod-product-compliance
Lightning Source LLC
Chambersburg PA
CBHW070123100426
42744CB00010B/1907